THE RULES FOR *Cats*

THE RULES FOR Cats

4,000-Year-Old Secrets for Controlling Your Owner

BY BRADFORD TELFORD AND MICHAEL CADER
ILLUSTRATIONS BY PETER SPACEK

CADER BOOKS

A DUTTON BOOK

DUTTON
Published by the Penguin Group
Penguin Books USA Inc., 375 Hudson Street,
New York, New York 10014, U.S.A.
Penguin Books Ltd, 27 Wrights Lane,
London W8 5TZ, England
Penguin Books Australia Ltd, Ringwood,
Victoria, Australia
Penguin Books Canada Ltd, 10 Alcorn Avenue,
Toronto, Ontario, Canada M4V 3B2
Penguin Books (N.Z.) Ltd, 182-190 Wairau Road,
Auckland 10, New Zealand

Penguin Books Ltd, Registered Offices:
Harmondsworth, Middlesex, England

First published by Dutton, an imprint of Dutton Signet, a division of
Penguin Books USA Inc.
Distributed in Canada by McClelland & Stewart Inc.

First Printing, February, 1997
10 9 8 7 6 5 4 3 2 1

Copyright © Cader Company Inc., 1997
All rights reserved

 REGISTERED TRADEMARK—MARCA REGISTRADA

LIBRARY OF CONGRESS CATALOGING-IN-PUBLICATION DATA is available

ISBN: 0-525-94362-5
Printed in the United States of America
Set in Bembo

COVER AND BOOK DESIGN BY CHARLES KRELOFF

This book is printed on acid-free paper

CONTENTS

Why the Rules Rule

The History of the Rules Cat Mystery *10*

The Contemporary Rules Cat Crisis *12*

So What Are the Rules for Cats? *15*

Meet Some Famous Rules Kitties *20*

But First the Product—You! *24*

And About this "Product" Thing *25*

Some Other "Original" Rules to Reconsider *27*

The Rules for Cats

1. Be a "Creature Unlike Any Other" *30*

2. And for God's Sake, Don't Come When
    They Call You *32*

3. Don't Act Like a Dog *36*

4. And Think Twice about Living
    with a Dog Owner *39*

5. Be Frisky, but Mysterious *40*

6. No More Than Casual Purring Most
    of the Time *44*

7. Don't Rush into Laps, and Other Rules
    for Intimacy *45*

8. And Always End Lap Sessions First *46*

9. Accentuate the Positive, and Other
    Rules for Adoptions *48*

10. Be Sickeningly Cute, and Other Rules for Kittens . .*49*

11. Naps Heal All Wounds—Coping with Spaying
    and Declawing *50*

12. Litter If You Don't Like Your Litter *52*

13. Be Finicky, but Not Too Finicky *53*

14. Don't Accept a Saturday Night Leftover after
    Wednesday *55*

15. Don't Eat Houseplants. And If You Do,
Be Discreet *57*

16. Don't Discuss Any of Your Other Eight Lives with
Your Owner *59*

17. Don't Screech, Don't Hiss, and Certainly Don't
Caterwaul *61*

18. A Nap Is Always More Than a Nap *63*

19. A Rules Nap Is Part Preparation… *65*

20. …and Part Location… *66*

21. …and Part Beautification… *68*

22. …and Always Perfectly Poised and Posed *69*

23. The Golden Rule of Clawing *72*

24. Sweaters, Bows, and Tiaras: Rules for Dealing
with Humiliating Costumes *73*

25. Into Each Life a Little Hair Must Fall:
Rules for Shedding *75*

26. Let Your Owner Be the Owner.
Most of the Time *77*

27. Love Only Those Who Love You. But
    Don't Love Them Too Much 78

28. Slowly Invite Your Owner into Your Family
    and Other Rules for Moms with Litters *79*

29. You're Number One: Rules for Dealing
    with the "Other Cat" *80*

30. A Rules Cat Watches Her Weight.
    But an Owner Watches It More *83*

31. Don't Get Lazy. Even If You've Got Bed,
    Couch, and Sock Drawer Privileges, You Still
    Need the Rules *85*

32. Don't Discuss the Rules with Your Psychiatrist . .*87*

33. Don't Be a Pill: Some Rules for Interacting
    with the Vet *90*

34. Break Lamps, Break Tchotchkes,
    but Don't Break the Rules *91*

35. Be a Creative Tail Chaser: Some Tips *92*

36. How to Play with String Without
    Debasing Yourself *94*

WHY
THE
RULES
Rule

THE HISTORY OF THE RULES CAT MYSTERY

*N*o one seems to remember how the Rules for Cats got started. While elephants never forget, Rules cats never let their *owners* forget. But experts do believe the Rules can be traced to Ancient Egypt's fabled Twentieth Dynasty of the thirteenth century B.C. After unsealing the massive tomb of Ramses II, who reigned over his Nile kingdom for an unprecedented 67 years (an incredible 1,072 cat years), archaeologists were amazed at their discovery. While the burial chambers contained what any Egyptologist would expect—gold and silver, sarcophagi and thrones, crooks, flails, ankhs, even a box of perfectly preserved Twinkies (shelflife 10,000 years)—the pharaoh's suite of rooms paled in comparison to the breathtaking beauty of the Royal Cat Chambers.

The treasures they found there boggled their imaginations—hand-carved wooden cat toys, sizable lengths of woven hemp string, even jewel-encrusted cat beds, beautifully lined with brilliantly intact shag carpeting. And there was jar after translucent, alabaster jar of 3,000-year-old pet supplies—myrrh-based Assyrian catnip, Hittite litter, an extraordinary collar of hammered gold and Persian turquoise (inscribed with an incantation to ward off fleas and scarab beetles), and almost a pound of cypress wood dust believed to be the original shavings from what must have been a magnificent royal scratching post.

The archaeologists knew the ancients worshiped cats (as well they should have). But they'd never seen anything like this before. They were particularly astonished to uncover a most remarkable set of hieroglyphs which, when translated, read:

Rule 24: Pharaoh, schmaraoh, he's still got to change your litter

The cat was out of the bag.

For 4,000 years owners have been fixated on and fascinated by their cats. You think this is an accident? Some trick of evolution? Luck? Think again. It's all because of the Rules for Cats, thirty-six simple steps to make you irresistible to your owner, be he pharaoh, pharmacist, or felon.

THE CONTEMPORARY RULES CAT CRISIS

*F*or centuries we Rules cats, from the temples of yore to the townhouses of today, have passed down the secrets and shared the magic of the Rules for Cats, doing what cats have done for each other since the world began.

But in this century, the life of the modern Rules cat has changed dramatically. Many have gone on to fame and fortune as actors, musicians, and corporate spokeskitties; and most notably, cats have advanced to become America's number-one household pet. Cats today are supposed to have nine exciting and fulfilling lives that have nothing whatsoever to do with their owners (and who can really *own* a cat, we ask?). Rules cats are independent, strong-willed, self-determining.

But let's face it—deep inside, if the truth be told, we really want the old-fashioned life of the cat. The laps, the naps, the rainy days inside (with the dog *outside*), and lots of tasty *saumon fumée*. And we all want to have our owners crazy about us. It's fun to be worshiped. Just ask the Aga Khan. Ask Sharon Stone.

So what can we say? The hectic pace of juggling all our lives and all our fabulous careers, as well as maintaining our cat's-pajamas status in America's homes, has taken its toll. Many of us have confused or forgotten the very basics that have made us objects of divine contemplation for 40 centuries.

Recently we ran into our friend Melanie at the vet, and she whispered, "Hey, I let my owner *end* the lap session first, right? Or is it the other way around? I also accepted last Saturday's table scraps *after* Wednesday. That's OK, isn't it? And last week I acted like a dog for a few minutes, just to see what my owner would do. He seemed to like it, although he's been calling me Rover lately."

Calling her *Rover?* Her name may as well be Spot.

We scratched our heads, we scratched the vet, we scratched that little patch behind our ears that never seems to stop itching, wondering what on earth to do. Cats across the country were ignorantly, negligently breaking the Rules for Cats, jeopardizing their status as true household gods and goddesses. Some cats were even coming when they were called. Something had to be done. And the pen, we decided, was mightier than the claw.

Today's cat needed help. It seemed that kitties all over had literally napped away all their memory of the

Rules for Cats. And those kitties needed a wake-up call!
So we got to work setting down the Rules for Cats on
paper for any animal who wanted to relearn the essen-
tials of laps and leftovers, of string-playing and
tail-chasing, of embodying "frisky" and living the
mystery.

But just as we were putting the final touches on this
tome, our public service announcement and our master-
piece, we saw those two women on *Jenny Jones*, talking
about those *other* "Rules" that have gotten so much
attention lately. And now we're here to tell you that, with
all apologies to those "authors" (and the hundreds of
thousands of women whose self-esteem they've systemat-
ically annihilated), the Rules for Cats have been around a
lot longer. About four millennia longer. So there.

SO WHAT ARE
THE RULES FOR CATS?

*O*ur owners wonder about us. They wonder why we sniff at seemingly delectable leftovers before turning up our noses and marching haughtily away. They wonder how we can strike unfathomably elegant napping poses time and time again. Our owners are even known to remark amongst themselves how they don't really *own* their cats, how their cats, in truth, thoroughly own *them,* and how this both delights and mystifies them. "Why," repeat the owners like so many Buddhist novices, "is this so?"

In four words: the Rules for Cats.

The ostensibly odd, unusual, irrational, quirky, inexplicable, and mysterious behavioral patterns for which cats are justly famous—and beloved—are not so much the product of millions of years of evolution and breeding as the Rules for Cats well executed. We behave in our peculiar, quixotic ways on purpose; it's all part of a divine and multifaceted plan. And we do these Rules so well we appear perfectly natural and wondrously feline when doing them. Kind of neat, huh?

And what's really interesting (apart from every aspect of a Rules cat) is how those other "Rules" pale in comparison to the beauty, grace, and eternal wisdom embedded in every single one of the Rules for Cats. Just take a gander at these:

COMPARE, CONTRAST	
OURS	**THEIRS**
Be frisky, but mysterious	Be honest but mysterious
Always end lap sessions first	Always end phone calls first
Don't accept a Saturday night leftover after Wednesday	Don't accept a Saturday night date after Wednesday
Break lamps, break tchotchkes, but don't break the Rules	Don't break the Rules

A reading of their "Rules" renders most people nervous and sweaty (at best) or calculating and self-loathing (at worst). Reading our Rules enlightens and informs kitties everywhere, all while demystifying the joys (and occasional noise) of Rules cat ownership.

Now try the following exercise using a brief excerpt from that other work. Every time you see the words "husband" and "man," simply substitute "owner." Each time you see "wife" or "woman," substitute "cat."

> If you didn't do *The Rules* at the begining of your relation-ship your husband might ignore you, talk to you rudely, or treat you badly....The same man who would act indifferent or ignore a wife who pursued him wouldn't dream of it with the woman who did *The Rules*.

Don't you see our point? Of course Rules cats are flattered that the "authors" of that other work think so highly of the Rules for Cats. It *is* a system by which Rules cats charm, enchant, captivate, and enrapture owners across the globe. But Rules cats are Rules cats, and women are women. Rules cats don't run for the Senate, chair major corporations, write some of the best literature of the past two centuries, or star on *Knots Landing.* And women (with the possible exception of Leona Helmsley) don't claw furniture or parade around with fresh kills hanging out of their mouths.

Is this so hard to understand?

We certainly hope not. But if any of your owners have started behaving strangely toward the men in their lives, if they've lost a great deal of weight and sleep, if they've had total nervous breakdowns and checked in to the nearest psychiatric ward, you'll know that they've read the Rules for Cats in its diluted form, *The Rules*. In this case, be extra nice to your owner. She needs all the help she can get. Meanwhile we'll try to do our part to stop the insanity and break the cycle of destruction.

Obviously some Rules-breaking Rules cat spilled the beans. And we're looking into it. We don't know if it was a feline owned by one of the "authors" of those other "Rules," or if it was an animal owned by one of their friends (although friends shouldn't let friends do *those* "Rules"). One theory has it that Fritz the Cat, that seventies icon and iconoclast, sold those "authors" a bootleg copy of the Rules for Cats to support his devastating catnip addiction. But so far Fritz's handlers have denied all charges, saying he cleaned himself up years ago.

In any event, we will not rest until we find the loose-lipped kitty culprit (but we might nap a little now and then). If you have any information that might lead to the capture of this traitor to Rules cats everywhere (and to women and men, for that matter), please call:

1-800-555-HISS

It's a confidential, toll-free call. And if you're a real Rules cat, your owner won't think twice of your using the phone (Rule 5: Be frisky, but mysterious).

MEET SOME FAMOUS
RULES KITTIES

*B*y doing the Rules for Cats you create a warm, soft spot in your owner's heart, not to mention his laundry hamper and his gym bag. If you religiously follow these thirty-six simple Rules (and any others you can think of—a Rules cat is always encouraged to make up new Rules, so long as we get our 10 percent) you will train your owner to worship the ground you walk on, to treat you like a creature unlike any other, to fluff your napping pillow, to freshen your litterbox, even to scratch your head no matter how many times you've scratched his coffee table. In the end, a Rules kitty always owns her owner.

But what comes next is up to you and the nine imaginations that go with your nine fabulous lives. The consummate Rules cat understands that while owner-ownership may be the first step, it certainly doesn't have to be the last. With the right amount of creativity and foresight (and perhaps the right agent, publicist, and masseuse) a Rules cat can journey from the humblest of chesterfields and ottomans to unfathomable heights of power, fame, and feline fortune. Just look at these Rules cats and their Rules cat success stories.

FELIX THE CAT
Everybody knows he had a bag of tricks. But did you know the bag was by Louis Vuitton? With a matching travel case and collar?

TONY THE TIGER
He's finicky, but not too finicky. Of course we don't recommend his diet for every Rules cat—the sugar, the sodium, the FD&C Yellow #5. But what about his visibility? His staying power? They're *grr-eat!*

THE PINK PANTHER
This cat's first Rule must read *be a feature unlike any other*, what with five motion pictures, exotic locations, sexy accents, enormous diamonds. Who could ask for more?

SYLVESTER
So he never got Tweety Bird. But have you seen his suite at the Beverly Wilshire?

GARFIELD
He may live with a dog, but this cat rules his roost like
no other. You can sum up his success in three easy
words: syndication, syndication, syndication.

THE LION KING
$400 million in domestic box office? Overseen by Jeffrey
*Katz*enberg? You do the math.

Some of you might bat a whisker at all these mega-
Rules kitties being cartoons. You might think they're
misrepresentative, flat, or two-dimensional. *Meoy-vay*—
we promise you happiness, security, a shot at global
cultural influence, and you kvetch about a third dimen-
sion? Doing the Rules for Cats is not about depth,
unless you're talking about cushions. But here are some
fleshed out Rules-rulers for all you purists.

THE EXXON TIGER
America puts a tiger in its tank while this tiger puts T-
bills in his. Puts William Blake to shame. Sure "Tiger,
Tiger" burned bright, but his copyright burned out.

THE MGM LION
He's the top
He's the most
He's got 12 percent of the gross.

THE MTM KITTEN
Sure Mary Tyler Moore went on to make *Ordinary People.* But her logo's little kitten was so sickeningly cute he retired to beachfront property in Boca Raton.

MORRIS THE CAT
Morris is the ultimate. He took one easy rule (Rule 13: Be finicky, but not too finicky) and parlayed it into a Q-rating that puts both Connie's and Maury's to shame.

Here are some other cats (and humans) that have followed, broken, or made up their own *Rules:*

HOBBES—Let Calvin be Calvin. Most of the time

TOM—Act like a professional (not like a carnivore) with Jerry

HELLO KITTY—Be frisky, but weirdly marketable

KITTY CARLISLE HART—Always be perfectly poised and posed

KITTY KELLY—The golden rule of clawing Nancy Reagan

BUT FIRST THE PRODUCT—YOU!

*I*t's so easy. All Rules cats are born with voluptuous fur coats that countless women (and even a few men) would die to wear while strolling up Madison Avenue. Whether long or short, solid, striped, or splotched, we've got the kind of fur that becomes *our* legend most. And no matter where you stand on the fur debate, a Rules cat fur coat is *always* politically unimpeachable (unlike Richard Nixon).

As serious as she is about her appearance, a Rules cat tries not to do her serious grooming in front of her owner. It's a private, Rules cat thing. So slip behind the curtains, go into an empty room, or crawl behind that warm washing machine or dryer and clean up lickety-split.

But since a Rules cat does want to let her owner know what she goes through to please him (and adhere to the laws of veterinary science), don't worry one little bit about horking up the occasional hairball. Your owner will understand. It's the small price you pay to please him. And it's a small price (and just a moderate-sized mess) he pays for being the lucky owner of you, a flawless Rules cat.

🐾

AND ABOUT THIS "PRODUCT" THING

*R*ules cats don't mind being "products." This is capitalism, after all. Mysterious, frisky, unattainable, and worthy of any owner's undying affection, Rules cats can be adopted for a nominal fee from shelters (or for no fee from numerous baskets and cardboard boxes). Many owners take advantage of breeders who offer exotic kitties at extreme prices. But what's money compared to the thrill of owning a creature unlike any other, of carrying debt unlike any other?

And Rules cats don't mind being commodified. We're Rules cats. We let owners believe in the myth of ownership because it makes them feel better:

Rule 26: Let your owner be the owner.
Most of the time

But in those other "Rules," the "authors" also referred to their readers as "products." And that's really gotten our dander up.

In the past hundred years women have gone from

suffragists to submarine commanders and beyond. And,
by golly, if women in 1997 start viewing themselves as
"products," by 1998 they'll start believing that "barefoot
and pregnant in the kitchen" is the sexiest phrase in the
English language. By 2000 they'll long for the days when
a bash over the head and a drag by the hair to the
nearest cave meant "Will you marry me?"

Yes, we've read our Jane Austen and our Camille
Paglia (many Rules cats are highly literate, and some
have tenure at major dog obedience schools). And yes,
there are factors of economy that play into many negoti-
ations of gender and politics. But someone needs to set
those "authors" straight about the difference between
"human" and "animal," between "woman" and "object,"
between "person" and "perversion." It's fine to be a
pretty woman. It's fine to watch *Pretty Woman*. But don't
buy in to the *Pretty Woman* myth. Of course you'll never
get paid as well as Julia Roberts. But at least you won't
be a hooker.

The point is, Rules cats *want* to be owned and there-
fore relish being commodified. But we don't need any
competion from women. And they've got their hands
full, too.

SOME OTHER "ORIGINAL" RULES TO RECONSIDER

THE TEN COMMANDMENTS

Look at where Moses & Co. were hanging out—a sandbox of biblical proportion. And then there's that "Thou shalt not worship false gods"—like dogs, goldfish, even golden calves. Add a "thou shalt worship Rules cats and the monotheistic deity of your choice" and you've got a real commandment.

MARTIN LUTHER'S 95 THESES

Pope Leo X was a notorious cat-hater who'd tried to round up all the Vatican's strays and do decidedly un-Christian things to them. Kind of makes you wonder.

THE DECLARATION OF INDEPENDENCE.

Independence. Need we say more?

"THE TWELVE DAYS OF CHRISTMAS"
Four calling birds
Three French hens
Two turtledoves
And a partridge in a pear tree.

All that yummy fowl! And a pear tree perfect for climbing! Who else could have written this?

"THIRTEEN WAYS OF LOOKING AT A BLACKBIRD"
Shame on you, Wallace Stevens. Only a Rules cat could look at a blackbird in that many imaginative ways.

CAT ON A HOT TIN ROOF
How about *Aardvark on a Hot Tin Roof*? Catchy, hmm?

And as for *Old Possum's Book of Practical Cats* and the subsequent musical, *Cats*, we're delighted to point out that Messrs. Eliot and Lloyd Webber are almost as good at hyping us as they are at hyping themselves.

THE
RULES
FOR
Cats

Rule 1

BE A "CREATURE UNLIKE ANY OTHER"

*S*o you're a cat. You've romped, you've frolicked, you've stretched, you've napped, all while pondering your coat, your claws, your essential catness. You read Rule 1 and say to yourself, *Felix, domestica,* what more could anyone want? You think you've got it licked. That it's in the bag.

Well, think again.

The Rules cat understands that being a creature unlike any other has little to do with mundane issues like genus and species. The Rules cat knows that what comes naturally is never enough. But the Rules cat also understands that being a creature unlike any other is not about being unusually cuddly, exceptionally furry, or particularly frisky. Frankly, it's all about breeding.

Not that the Rules Kitty needs an impeccable pedigree. Some of the best Rules cats have come from some of the worst places—pounds, alleys, Thai restaurants. But breeding, as any Rules cat knows, is no mere matter of blue ribbons, ancient bloodlines, and symmetrical whiskers. It's just good old-fashioned style.

You walk (aesthetically), purr (furtively), and stare (majestically). You do not clean yourself; you beautify a planet. You do not take a nap; you fulfill a prophetic dream. The Rules cat doesn't so much sit on the couch as complete its artistic possibility. You leap on the coffee table, strike a classic pose, and suddenly an image worthy of any Impressionist appears as if by magic.

It doesn't matter that you don't know who your father is and that your mother ate one of your siblings. You're a Rules cat. You're pet enough for even the pickiest of owners. But are they owner enough for *you?*

They'd better be. Because, no matter what, the Rules cat's owner believes his cat is the most flawless, fascinating thing ever to come along in fur and four legs. And the Rules cat agrees. Of course everyone has bad days. But even if you're feeling somewhat out of sorts, if you're worried about mange, fleas, ticks, or any of the innumerable afflictions that plague contemporary catdom, you never let it show. Being a Rules cat is not about being yourself. It's about following the Rules.

Rule 2
AND FOR GOD'S SAKE, DON'T COME WHEN THEY CALL YOU

*O*wners have always called their cats. And for 4,000 years cats always knew exactly what to do: nothing. But in the 1960s, as cats all across the nation began speaking out for equal rights while burning their collars and letting their coats grow long and unwashed, something terrible began to happen—owners called, and cats came.

Of course it was a time of great social upheaval. The home was no longer the safe haven it was during the Eisenhower era, when cats luxuriated on commodious sills and cushiony chairs (and dogs stayed out in the yard, thank you). By 1968 the American living room had Janis Joplin on the stereo, hippies on the TV, and dogs, cats, snakes, lizards, gerbils, even Sea Monkeys, vying for space, recognition, and table scraps. The very word "cat" became synonymous with all kinds of friendly, accessible creatures like the generic "cool cat," the folksy Cat Stevens, even Josie and her litter of musical Pussycats.

Cats came down from their pedestals (and other comfy places) to protest the dogs of war, advocate catnip legalization, and make peace with their fellow household residents. It was a great time in cat history, and the Rules cat must never forget to thank that generation of cats who so boldly forsook comfort, luxury, and convenience for what really mattered.

But the Rules cat knows what really matters today. In the sixties cats forfeited their mystery, and without mystery cats are creatures like *so* many others. What matters now is making the return to mystery, playing hard to get, following the Rules. And the Rules are crystal clear—don't come when they call you. For God's sake.

If you do, you'll simply train your owner to *expect* things from you, like responses, sticks, and newspapers. Sure, you want to train your owner. But you must train him the right way. Like the Woodhouse way.

🐈

Time for a Little Quiz

*T*he Rule is pretty clear. Don't come when they call you. Just Say No. Just Don't Do It. So here's a little quiz. And since these are pluralistic, multicultural times, we've thrown in a few curves.

1. Your owner returns from a weekend away and calls out, "Here, Rufus." You:

    A. Tear into the living room, leap up on your owner and cover him with wet, sloppy kisses and licks.

    B. Slither coyly up to your owner and "sniff" him with your forked tongue.

    C. Roll your eyes, flex your nictating membrane, and resume your nap.

2. Your owner's preparing some salmon and calls out, "Here Camille, you want a snacky-wacky?" You:

    A. Bound into the kitchen, sit up, and beg.

    B. Screech loudly, flap your wings, and respond in English.

    C. Roll your eyes, flex your nictating membrane, and resume your nap.

3. *Your owner slips, falls, breaks his leg, and cries out,*
"Peaches!" You:
> A. Lie down next to him and whimper
> sympathetically.
> B. Mount your Habitrail wheel and scamper.
> C. Roll your eyes, flex your nictating membrane, and
> resume your nap on your owner's warm, immobilized
> chest.

Extra Credit

What's *nictating*?
> A. The highly addictive chemical compound found
> in catnip.
> B. A professional Rules cat term that roughly means,
> "toying with a mouse, moth, or any other annoyance."
> C. The fabulous designer sheath across a cat's eye that
> acts like a second eyelid.

Rule 3
DON'T ACT LIKE A DOG

*R*ules Cats follow the Rules. That's why they're creatures unlike any other. And why they never, ever, *ever* act like a dog. Remember that dogs are pets, cats are family, and Rules cats, unlike Princess Diana, are still royalty.

There's a cat we know whose life is the envy of all her friends. Her real estate holdings alone are the stuff of catnip hallucinations—a Fifth Avenue pied-à-terre (fabulous views from fabulous window seats); oceanfront property in East Hampton (some kitties have litterboxes, this kitty has a litterbeach); and a significant estate in New Jersey's hunt country (significant chintz, significant armchairs). It's enough to make even the most rigorous Rules cat froth at the mouth. But Rules cats don't catch rabies. The only froth in a Rules cat's mouth is the froth of freshly prepared steamed milk (do the Rules and all this can be yours!).

What's more, this cat's owner discusses her as if she were a favorite daughter. He glowingly comments on

What's wrong with this picture?

her every idiosyncrasy; he oohs and ahhs over her littlest friskiness. And would you now like to know this astonishingly lucky cat's name?

Dog.

Because she acts like one.

Don't roll over, don't play dead, and don't start wagging your tail. There's a lesson to be learned here. Dog acts like a dog. Dog comes when she's called. Dog shakes. Dog fetches. Dog even lets her owner put a leash on her and walk her through Central Park.

You can see where this is leading. Soon Dog's owner will feed her Alpo, have her catch Frisbees, ask her to lift her leg when she pees. And you can bet your litterbox that one day he's going to call her a bitch. And all because Dog doesn't follow the Rules. Actually, Dog can't even read. Perhaps that's her real problem.

Remember Dog. But don't act like Dog. And don't act like a dog.

Rule 4

AND THINK TWICE ABOUT LIVING WITH A DOG OWNER

*I*t's a dog-eat-dog world. Sometimes it's even a dog-eat-cat world. That's why a Rules cat should think twice before living with dog owners. Dogs, when they're not threatening a Rules cat's basic existence, are always noisy, sloppy, and given to fits. Unless your owner's a Ross Perot supporter or a Branch Davidian, these qualities will distract him unduly from his worshipping you.

And if your owner *does* support Ross Perot, you might want to consider comforting him with a giant scratching sound or comforting yourself by giving yourself up for adoption.

🐈

Rule 5

BE FRISKY,
BUT MYSTERIOUS

*M*uch of the Rules for Cats is about delaying
your personal gratification. The Rules take
willpower, fortitude, and extraordinary kitty character.
Doing the Rules is not doing what comes naturally,
doing what you want, doing what feels good. It's doing
the Rules. You want your owner to respect, fear, and
even worship you (think Egypt, think China, think
Elvis). A Rules cat never forgets that worship takes
restraint.

But friskiness is another matter entirely. Owners love
it when their Rules kitties are frisky, so long as they're
clever, inventive, and mysterious about it.

What better way to reinforce your own sense of self-
worth and your owners' sense of wonder and awe than
by flying through the dining room, let's say, between the
soup and the sorbet courses at a dinner party for 12
(replete with in-laws and bosses) with your owner's

leopard-print thong or bankruptcy papers hanging triumphantly from your Rules cat mouth?

But a Rules cat should save most stunts of this magnitude for when her owner's not there. When the owner is present, the timeworn activities in the Frisky Canon will more than suffice. You don't want to intimidate your owner by letting him know that you are, in fact, much more intelligent than he is. So stick to moth-chasing, string-playing, and toe-nibbling when he's there, and be the good little domestic kitty he knows you are.

But when he's asleep, not looking, or gone, become the Fantasy Rules cat he wants you to be. He'll think you're a real tiger. Just be careful with electrical appliances near the bathtub.

Frisky Business

*H*ere are some other frisky scenarios. Feel free to follow them directly, mix and match, or come up with your very own!

THE BEST TIME	PLACE	AND PROP
Midnight to six A.M.	Master bedroom	One or both owners
Midnight to six A.M.	Living room	Bang, Olufsen
Six A.M.	Kitchen	Stemware, flatware, Tupperware
Ten A.M.	Laundry room	Sheets, towels, fresh out of the dryer
Noon	Garage	Hardware
Two P.M.	Computer room	Hardware, software
Four P.M.	Garden	Small fauna, expensive flora
Six P.M.	Library	Reading lamps, newspapers, cocktail tumblers
Eight P.M.	Bathroom	Shampoo, perfume, and Xanax bottles
Ten P.M.	Guest bedroom	Guest

And here are some other "special occasions"
where the perfect Rules cat gesture will always
be remembered.

Weddings and wakes
Seders and shiva
Brisses, bar mitzvahs, bachelor and birthday parties
Family discussions, family quarrels
Interviews, intermission, intercourse

Rule 6
NO MORE THAN CASUAL PURRING MOST OF THE TIME

*O*wners love a challenge. And if they know they can get you going like an outboard motor with the offhand scratch, stroke, or rub, they'll lose interest. When you purr, you *want* to purr like a Harley-Davidson. But a Rules cat, on most occasions, purrs with no more enthusiasm than a small appliance. Like this vibrating pager, perhaps?

Rule 7
DON'T RUSH INTO LAPS, AND OTHER RULES FOR INTIMACY

*W*hen is it okay to claim your owner's lap as your own? The rule often varies depending on your disposition and your owner's schedule, not to mention the size, shape, consistency, and mean temperature of the lap in question as well as the natural fiber content of the clothes covering said lap.

If you're a kitten of three months a quick jump-and-claw session lasting no more than 30 seconds should more than suffice. If you're a three-year-old recent adoptee with a penchant for denim or khaki, a three-hour afternoon lapfest may be just a good start. But you're a Rules cat. If your owner loves you (and what owner wouldn't love *you*?), he'll respect whatever decision you make.

But the general rule is that in the beginning, a little lap goes a long way. Nothing makes an owner more thoughtless than thinking they've earned their cat's trust. A Rules cat can give a mouse, a bird, even a hairball, to her owner, but never her trust.

Rule 8
AND ALWAYS END
LAP SESSIONS FIRST

*Y*ou can't really own a lap. But you can *rule* a lap. Sometimes the owner's life is almost as complicated as the Rules cat's (although it's never nearly as aesthetically appealing or disarmingly mysterious). And while most owners would love to go days on end with

laps full of Rules cats, an owner must, at times, get up. Then his lap disappears.

Think about it. If your owner's a film buff, he goes to the movies rather than watching them on the VCR (a first-rate napping location—see Rule 18). If your owner is a Yankees or Cowboys fan, he'll probably stand up to cheer. And if he's a beer drinker, his glass will often be less than half empty (and his bladder *always* more than half full).

A well-trained owner can be relied upon for anything. But there's no such thing as a well-trained lap.

A True Fall from Grace

The vanishing lap conundrum. It's an eternal question, much like Larry King's suspender (and ex-wife) collection. One legend has it that the first Rules cat spent its first six days coiled up in man's lap, and when man got up on the seventh day to discover fire, invent the wheel, or buy a lottery ticket, the first Rules cat didn't realize what was happening until it was too late. The kitty didn't even land on its feet.

Rule 9
ACCENTUATE THE POSITIVE, AND OTHER RULES FOR ADOPTIONS

The adoption process is where the Rules cat really shines. Whether she's a six-week-old kitten in a wicker basket or a four-year-old stray in an ASPCA shelter, the Rules kitty knows that she's the One. She's confident, smart, sexy, demure, enigmatic, and totally free of ringworm. Her coat is clean, her eyes are bright, and even if she's got six toes, they're six Rules cat toes. She's not concerned in the least with the other cats around her. And she's not at all interested in her prospective owner. Besides, everybody knows that owners don't adopt Rules cats. Rules cats adopt owners.

Rule 10

BE SICKENINGLY CUTE, AND OTHER RULES FOR KITTENS

*B*aby owners tend to look like Eisenhower, Churchill, or baked hams, and baby Rules cats look like kittens. Need we say more?

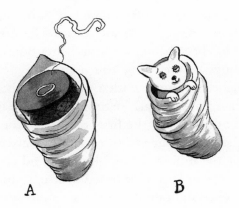

A Rules kitten never hams it up.

Rule 11

NAPS HEAL ALL WOUNDS— COPING WITH SPAYING AND DECLAWING

*E*very cat knows That Feeling. You're at the tail end of an idyllic kittenhood. You've reveled in your owner's bed, you've capered in her flower bed. You've played with yarn, grown frightened of yarn, forgotten about yarn, and played with yarn again. The first six months of life have been beautiful. Kittenhood always is.

But things are changing. You've probably had your first traumatic encounter with a vacuum cleaner or a rocking chair. And you are beginning to sense in your heart (and other places) the first stirrings of romance. Odors are stronger. Fur is sleeker. If you live with another cat, the innocent roughhousing and wrestling of kittenhood might have blossomed overnight into full-blown cat love. And one day, some six short months into your carefree life, you get That Feeling.

That Feeling?—it's like dread, but worse. You're

picked up, put in a box, tossed in the backseat, and driven to a cold, impersonal, severely lit place where you are drugged, snipped, sutured, and stitched in as much time as it takes Dick Morris to, well, never mind that. It all happens so fast you barely know what's hit you. But you are certain of one thing. The life of the kitten has ended.

But the life of the Rules cat has just begun! Neutering may close one door, but, for the Rules kitty it opens countless others. So don't resist. You're a Rules cat, and Rules cats don't resist what owners try to do to them. Besides, you are so busy pleasing and mystifying your owner, you'd never have time for kids. So use your recuperation period to do something nice for yourself. Take an extra (aesthetically pleasing) nap. Take another. And always remember that most owners don't want a rowdy tom or hot-and-bothered female around the house.

As for claws, Rules cats know their claws mean independence, self-reliance, and protection in the great outdoors. But who really needs all that when you have the Rules For Cats?

Rule 12
LITTER IF YOU DON'T LIKE YOUR LITTER

*A*s far as the litterbox polemic goes, remember Rule 1. You are a creature unlike any other, an impeccably clean and well-groomed creature. You are *not* a maid. Besides, you have neither the body strength nor the opposable thumbs for this job.

Remember that in litterbox situations, things can go from interstate rest stop to Calcutta bus station in a very short time. So leave your owner a convenient reminder of his neglected obligation on any clean pillow, rug, or kitchen counter.

Rule 13
BE FINICKY,
BUT NOT TOO FINICKY

*C*ats (Rules and otherwise) are finicky. Cats have this bizarre mixture of the senses that is one-third touch, one-third taste, one-third smell. It's one of those oddities, like purring, gravity, and Steven Seagal's film career, that science cannot fully explain.

And the challenge-loving owner doesn't want it explained. He only wants to satisfy you, his mysterious, lovable Rules cat, and reaffirm his status as Rules cat protector, servant, and caterer. If you never let your

owner think he can satisfy you, he'll try so hard that you'll always be satisfied!

So don't scarf, snarf, or pig out. That's for dogs and other non-Rules species like Rush Limbaugh. And never clean your plate. Even if you're famished, let part of your meal go uneaten. It keeps your owner on his toes in his vigilant quest to satisfy you.

Generally, you should always remember that while the cat did eat the canary, the Rules cat had it served to her on a bed of fresh greens.

Rule 14

DON'T ACCEPT A SATURDAY NIGHT LEFTOVER AFTER WEDNESDAY

*S*aturday night. Dinner party. Tuna steak—fabulous. The salmon tartare—out of this world. Even the salad looked pretty good. Anchovies. And all your owner's friends were dazzled by your charm, your style, and your alluring good looks. You were the star of the evening. The owner's date paled in comparison to you. She even left early. Allergies (she said).

If your owner appreciates you, you'll start eating the fruits of your labors the next morning, or even that very night. But if a full day goes by, drop a few hints—sit on the fridge, purr a little louder (like an electric tooth-brush), or be extra considerate with your friskiness (knock only two picture frames off the mantel rather than the customary twelve). One of these should do the trick.

But once Wednesday's come and gone, it's time to practice the art of elegant refusal. You are finicky, and

you've got a reputation to protect. When your owner
serves you the Rules–violating plate, simply sniff, scoff,
and skedaddle. Then feel free to wreak a little frisky
havoc. If he's a painter, go to work on his favorite canvas.
If he's a writer, shred his latest novel.

Rule 15
DON'T EAT HOUSEPLANTS.
AND IF YOU DO, BE DISCREET

*E*ven the strongest Rules kitty can be tempted. And in most homes temptation comes in three guises: ficus, begonia, and philodendron.

It's an age-old dilemma. Your owner wants lush, full-bodied foliage to beautify and oxygenate his home, but you still need your roughage. What's more, you deserve your roughage. And since discretion is the better part of Rules kitty valor, here are some tips.

• Focus on the side that faces the wall. What your owner can't see won't harm him (or implicate you). He may wonder who gave his Boston fern an asymmetrical haircut. But you're a Rules cat. Keep him guessing.

• Go after the sick and the ailing. Put them out of their misery. But avoid rare orchids and bonsai trees.

• Consider yourself an artist. Topiary is all the rage these days. Try some abstract shapes and then move on to self-portraits.

But always be careful and watch what you eat. Many household plants are poisonous to cats, Rules and otherwise.

Rule 16
DON'T DISCUSS ANY OF YOUR OTHER EIGHT LIVES WITH YOUR OWNER

*A*gain, it's the mystery and not the history for Rules cats. Just because you always land on your feet doesn't mean you're obliged to talk about it. Your owner wants to fantasize about you in exotic locales and surreal situations. If he knows that you spent last night trapped in the garbage can hunting for the leftovers you refused on Wednesday, he'll start taking you for granted.

So let your owner dream on. Even if your other lives have proved relatively uneventful, keep quiet about it. Let him think you've been an Egyptian deity, a palace rat-catcher, a Tsarina's confidant, or Shirley MacLaine's bed warmer. And if your owner ever asks you directly, bat your tail three times in rapid succession, the Rules kitty's way of saying, "Don't go there."

Some Semantic Rules

*S*peaking of "don't go there," Rules cat owners should avoid the following puns. They're tired, they're dull, they're even slightly offensive.

Catastrophe (an unfortunate association)

Cataclysm (ditto)

Catalepsy (again)

Catarrh (a dry cough? that's not very nice)

Catamaran (the water problem)

Cataract (water again—and the blindness thing)

Catapult (we shudder to think)

Catamite (pederasty? blech)

Catatonic (unless you're talking about Al Gore)

Catalog (unless it's Neiman's or Horchow)

Catechism (*The Rules for Catholics*—not really our bag)

Rule 17

DON'T SCREECH, DON'T HISS, AND CERTAINLY DON'T CATERWAUL

*N*ot that you never, but the Rules cat generally tries not to. Even the most devoted Rules cat owner will shrink away in horror if you remind him of P.J. Harvey or a spat in the Clinton White House. Besides, a good, direct meow is always the preferred

mode of communication in most situations. But if you
fear for your sanctity or safety, a solitary screech is
certainly appropriate. If a dog, vacuum cleaner, or other
predator backs you into a corner, the dramatic and
inspired hiss (think Nora Desmond, think Blanche
Dubois, think Harvey Fierstein) is sure to get the right
kind of attention. And if that unknowable (and usually
unneutered) mood overtakes you, feel free to caterwaul.
Just try to do it like Domingo (or out of earshot). A
Rules cat wants flowers and catnip thrown at her. Not
shoes.

Rule 19
A RULES NAP IS PART PREPARATION . . .

*D*on't nap off the cuff (or paw). Plan your Rules naps for when your owner will be home and most likely to appreciate your physical and visual otherness. And don't worry if other cats have cuter tails, pinker noses, and softer tummies. Even the homeliest of strays turns into a pulchritudinous pussy when doing the Rules. And don't fret if you really don't feel like a catnap. The Rules for Cats isn't about how you feel, it's about (all together now) doing the Rules.

Rule 20
...AND PART LOCATION...

*N*ever worry about sleeping around. Your owner likes that about you. But don't do it in unattractive, unsavory, unimpressive, or undetectable areas. The floor is fine, but a Rules cat knows how to lie down so that the rug's pattern and her fur coat match up perfectly. If you love the refrigerator's meat and vegetable drawers,

that's perfectly acceptable. But don't nap there. Nap in a dresser drawer. Your owner will love your warming up his undies. And the fridge is too cold for anything other than intermittent friskiness (but beware the evil refrigerator door). And don't nap in nasty environments like under the kitchen sink or near the toilet. Your owner will associate you with scouring powder, garbage, or worse.

When you nap, pick places that are unusual, if not outlandish. Tufted ottomans and telephone books are good for starters, but a Rules cat uses her imagination. Try the piano, the kitchen counter, the Tiffany lampshade. There's a Rules cat we know who, as a kitten, took her first Rules nap in her owner's baseball mitt. A brilliant maneuver—feline suppleness met America's favorite pastime. He's worshiped her ever since.

Rule 21
...AND PART
BEAUTIFICATION...

*Y*ou owner may not want to watch you groom. He may only want to admire the results. Rules cats don't seriously groom themselves in front of their owners. We save that for our precious private time.

But, as is the case with the hairball pointer, your owner needs to know what kind of effort you take and what kind of time you spend in order to look your best *for him*. So when you're about to begin a Rules catnap, groom yourself for a few moments before you assume the complete position. Not only will 100 precise, practiced licks make you feel better about yourself, it'll also buff and fluff your coat to give you that extra napping edge.

Rule 22
...AND ALWAYS PERFECTLY POISED AND POSED

*P*ose and the world poses with you. Plotz and you plotz alone. Here are three of the classic Rules catnapping postures.

The Calico Croissant

The Siamese Centerfold

The New York Public Library Lion

Rules from All Over

*R*ules cats make the Rules. And you should perceive the Rules for Cats as a basic set ideal for any owner. But each owner is special (though not as special as his cat) and inevitably requires some Rules specific to him and him alone. If, for instance, your owner is an exercise freak, you might add something like "Rule 37: Watch out for the treadmill." Or if your owner frequently takes you traveling with him, you might consider, "Rule 38: The bear went over the mountain, but the Rules cat went first-class."

Here are some personalized rules that certain Rules kitties have shared with us recently. Perhaps they'll give you some ideas on how to begin creating the right rules for your particular situation.

FRANZ (Helmut Khol's calico)
Rule 74: Don't worry about leftovers. There won't be any

NORMAN (Itzhak Perlman's manx)
Rule 42: Relax. Those strings are *not* catgut

DISRAELI (Margaret Thatcher's tabby)
Rule 56: Even if your owner answers to "Baroness,"
never answer to "Princess"

OTTO (Clarence Thomas's Himalayan)
Rule 172: Don't shed on Coke cans

MR. ROURKE (Aaron Spelling's Persian)
Rule 87: What to do when there are more rooms in
the house than you can physically shed in

COCO (Ru Paul's Abyssinian)
Rule 95: What to do when it's your *owner* who's the
"creature unlike any other"

AGNES (Julia Ormond's mixed breed)
Rule 67: What to do when your owner's career is
over faster than your dinner

Rule 23
THE GOLDEN RULE OF CLAWING

*I*t's pretty simple. Avoid any object whose replacement cost exceeds the price of a standard declawing. Everything else is open season.

So be smart. You want the Louis XV settee, you settle for the beanbag chair. You crave the Chanel suit, you go after the warmup suit. You're hungry for the Chippendale leg, so hunker down on your owner's.

🐈

Rule 24
SWEATERS, BOWS, AND TIARAS: RULES FOR DEALING WITH HUMILIATING COSTUMES

*W*hen Christmas comes and it's time for that ridiculous getup your owner knitted for you, the *natural* thing to do is bolt and hide under the dryer until January 1. But the Rules cat is not natural. The Rules cat knows that owners get a real sadistic kick out of small cruelties like jingle-bells and sequin appliques. Owners are only human, after all.

So allow yourself to be tarted up like a pet-store mannequin and photographed repeatedly by inebriated aunts and uncles—whether it's a stovepipe hat for President's Day, a star-spangled bow for July 4, or Queen Esther's crown for Purim. You want to please your owner, indulge him, let him have his little fantasy. Sure, it might disgust you. But you can always nap and bear it.

Never forget what a certain dumb-looking head-piece did for the Cat in the Hat's career. And always remember Rule 23. If it's not terribly expensive (and if it's not, how *dare* they!), assert yourself and commit an act of old-fashioned defiance—invoke your retribution claws.

Rule 25

INTO EACH LIFE A LITTLE HAIR MUST FALL: RULES FOR SHEDDING

*H*air is a Rules cat's calling card. It lets everyone in the household know that while you might seem aloof and inaccessible, you really do care. Of course sometimes it is difficult to explain this sentiment when your owner's computer shorts out or the meatloaf looks as if it needs a shave, but give it time. Your owner worships you and will learn to relish even the tiniest, most pervasive aspects of your physical being.

But you've got to keep it interesting. You are a creature unlike any other; you shed more than Ted Danson in a sauna. Even as you read this, you've probably already hit two chairs, a sweater, and several legs. But a Rules kitty always remembers the toothbrush, the fruit basket, and the Steinway baby grand. What about a new centerpiece for the dining room table? And a Rules cat delights in helping his owner with his wardrobe, so spend some time figuring out which hairs would look best on your owner's suede jacket, his linen suit, even his face.

No matter what you decide, just remember that the only bad kind of hair is no hair (otherwise they might forget about you).

Rule 26
LET YOUR OWNER BE THE OWNER. MOST OF THE TIME

A Rules cat should let her owner think *he's* the owner, the one in charge, the leader, the more highly evolved species. Of course Rules cats are aware of their superiority. But doing the Rules is about denying who and what you are. Kind of sad, huh?

Of course, a Rules cat is not a sad and misguided Rules girl. A Rules cat occasionally puts her paw down.

Rule 27

LOVE ONLY THOSE WHO LOVE YOU. BUT DON'T LOVE THEM TOO MUCH

*O*f course you love your owner. And perhaps you love his family and even a few of his friends. But remember that in any relationship there's the "lover" and the "beloved." Do we need to clarify?

A Rules cat is capable of love, so long as she does not break, bend, or even stretch the Rules. Love your owner by getting him to love you more (by doing the Rules), not by making outlandish displays or gestures. Just look at our tango-loving friend. She looks like Al Pacino or Tom Jones. Cute, but tacky. And the next thing you know, she'll be featured with the Ringling Brothers or on "Stupid Pet Tricks."

Rule 28

SLOWLY INVITE YOUR OWNER INTO YOUR FAMILY AND OTHER RULES FOR MOMS WITH LITTERS

*W*hatever you do, don't allow your owner to handle your kids before you're darn good and ready. And don't let him give them up for adoption until they're weaned. Remember that the joys of motherhood are second only to the joys of doing the Rules for Cats. Your owner may stress about all these new mouths to feed (and give away), but give him time. A brood of kittens can be a marvelous asset when it comes to passively beating your owner into a drooling, sentimental submission to your every whim. Again, it's that "sickeningly cute" quality.

So if you're at all able (and if Rule 11 doesn't apply), go find the nearest tom and knock yourself out! And up!

Rule 29

YOU'RE NUMBER ONE: RULES FOR DEALING WITH THE "OTHER CAT"

*W*hen you share your owner with another cat, you probably *feel* like making friends. It's another warm body for lounging on, after all, and it's even furry. But the Rules cat's affection is nothing unless it's hard-earned. So you restrain yourself with that other "animal" and maintain a polite feline detente. At least for a while.

Sometimes tensions between you and the "other cat" can build to a breaking point, what with limited couch and sill space. The Rules cat finds a way to resolve the conflict peacefully lest a cat fight occur. Cat fights are definitely not the Rules. They're *Melrose Place* or *Dynasty*.

But if the "other cat" happens to be a Rules kitty, too, then do the Rules together. Two Rules cats are always better (and more merciless) than one.

A Note to Socks: Some Special Rules for a Second Term

Rule 1: Be a bipartisan creature unlike any other

Rule 2: Make an ass of yourself, but don't act like an elephant

Rule 3: Come when they call you, otherwise you'll get subpoenaed

Rule 4: And watch where you're shedding—you might incriminate yourself

Rule 5: Just because Chelsea's matriculating doesn't mean she doesn't love you anymore

Rule 6: Try horking a hairball to the twenty-first century

Rule 7: Don't sit in on cabinet meetings, just sit on cabinets

Rule 8: No matter how the president treats him, George Stephanopulos is not your scratching post

Rule 9: 2,001 regulations on playing with red tape

Rule 10: Break laws, but don't break the Rules

Rule 30
A RULES CAT WATCHES HER WEIGHT. BUT AN OWNER WATCHES IT MORE

*K*now what your owner likes, and then do it. Some owners appreciate a sleek physique. If this is your owner, take your cue from Claudia, Naomi, and Kate, career gals who, by the way, do their best work on *catwalks*. The high-minded professionals of the fashion industry have named one of their most important business resources after you and the mysterious way you strut your stuff. So go easy on the tuna and be sure to get plenty of exercise between naps. Your owner will appreciate the hard work you put into staying slim, almost as much as he appreciates not having to cope with cracked ribs every time you jump on his chest.

On the other hand (for all you fat cats out there), when a Rules cat packs 10 or 15 extra pounds there really *is* more of her to love. Many owners prefer a cat who looks like Liz Taylor during her John Warner phase. And when you weigh as much as a small car, your owner will think twice before attempting to extract you from any "off-limits" napping locations, especially if he's got a disk problem.

So be sensitive to your owner—thin may be in, or fat where it's at.

Celery or fudge? Let your owner be the judge.

Rule 31

DON'T GET LAZY. EVEN IF YOU'VE GOT BED, COUCH, AND SOCK DRAWER PRIVILEGES, YOU STILL NEED THE RULES

*I*t's every Rules cat's nightmare. You've kept lap time at a minimum, you've been frisky *and* mysterious, you've never come when they've called you, and you've always napped with curves that put Modigliani to shame.

But perhaps you've been purring too much, or too loudly. Maybe you accepted Saturday's filet mignon on *Thursday* morning. Maybe you gobbled up your owner's favorite fern with no sense of artistic integrity, God forbid.

Suddenly you find yourself banished from your favorite wing chair. One day you realize your favorite window seat has a brand new fax machine on it. Or you wake up from a nap to see your owner come through the door with a cocker spaniel puppy. *Ick.*

The point is that you've worked hard to dominate your owner and one or two slipups can reduce your status from object of profound meditation and reverence to common housecat. And while there's lots about Tonya Harding and Joan Collins that is, there is *nothing* common about a Rules cat.

🐾

Rule 32
DON'T DISCUSS THE RULES WITH YOUR PSYCHIATRIST

*W*e live in complicated times; we live nine complicated lives. With the plight of the Hutus and the
Tutsis, the Bosnians and the Serbs, New York's homeless
and New York's Jets, a Rules cat must always show extra
affection when her owner shells out for a dozen sessions
with the cat shrink at $80 a pop. So go ahead and rub up
against your owner's leg a bit more often. Hang out in
the lap for an extra five or ten minutes. And feel free to
pure a little louder than the Rules suggest (instead of
"vibrating pager" try for "blender set on purée").

And by all means let your psychiatrist into certain
parts of your numerous lives. Discuss your kitty litter
issues. Explore your fears about the rocking chair, the
vacuum cleaner, about being trapped forever in the hall
closet. Your cat psychiatrist is concerned about you; he
wants you to be happy (for $80 an hour, many people
would want you to be happy).

Among your psychiatrist's many recommendations will probably be extra naps, more personal time, and a thorough reading of *Meditations for Cats Who Do Too Much*. Listen to your doctor. But not too much. And never, ever discuss the Rules for Cats with him. The reasons are fairly simple.

Some psychiatrists will try to tell you the Rules for Cats are dishonest and manipulative. They'll lecture you that these are *human* qualities, that they're most unbecoming for cats. They'll encourage you to be more open with your feelings, more trusting, more loving. That, of course, is their solution for everything, and it's all great advice for dealing with family, friends, and the occasional throw rug. And it's swell for neurotic people, too. But not for cats. A Rules cat is a creature unlike any other, not some lovey-dovey furball schmuck.

Most shrinks don't know how difficult it is to train an owner. They have no clue how much planning it takes to groom our owners to heed, to obey, to worship. If psychiatrists knew what we go through, they would recommend that we focus on ourselves instead and not try to make things happen on some timetable. But fresh litter must happen on a timetable. *Our* timetable.

Another reason for not telling your psychiatrist about the Rules for Cats is that you want to avoid the to-Rules-or-not-to-Rules argument with him. Why? Because you'd win. And think how inferior your psychiatrist would feel. Then again, your shrink's already a *cat* therapist. How much lower can he go? Hamster healer?

Rule 33
DON'T BE A PILL:
SOME RULES FOR INTERACTING
WITH THE VET

*Y*ou may not mind it, you may hate it. But a Rules
cat needs her regular checkups. You will have to go
to the vet, and how you react to this inevitability has a
lot to do with your disposition. All we can say is relax,
breathe deeply, and chill out.

Besides, certain people have designed both straitjackets and muzzles for the neurotic Rules cat patient.
And we don't care if Gucci or Prada designs them,
muzzles are for dogs. And straitjackets for cuckoos.

Rule 34

BREAK LAMPS, BREAK TCHOTCHKES, BUT DON'T BREAK THE RULES

*S*ure, doing the Rules for Cats is a lot of work. It can stress out even the hardiest of Rules kitties. So, if you really need to, go ahead and let your demon-cat out of her bag. Break everything in the house that your owner hasn't cat-proofed. You'll have a great time, and he (and his insurance company) will chalk up the damage to the frisky mystique.

Rule 35
BE A CREATIVE TAIL CHASER: SOME TIPS

*E*very Rules cat knows that after the first 650 times the tail-chasing thing gets a bit old. But owners thrive on it and expect it on a regular basis. Since the Rules cat wants to please her owner (but, again, not too much) no matter how boring the task, here are some scenarios that might relieve some of the tedium.

Political

The Bill: You're the 49th president; your tail is an Arch Deluxe.

The Whitewater: You're Kenneth Starr; your tail is something no one really understands or cares about.

The Gore: Your tail is a personality.

The Gingrich: Your tail is 1994.

The Yeltsin: You're drunk; who's that cute kitty in front of you?

Entertainment

The Letterman: Your tail hates you. You hate you. The pathos is rather disturbing.

The Martha Stewart: Have your staff do the chasing.

The Barbra Streisand: Your tail is a manicure unlike any other.

The Keanu Reeves: Dude, your tail is an enigma.

The Michael Jackson: Marry me, baby; just don't make me touch you.

Rule 36
HOW TO PLAY WITH STRING WITHOUT DEBASING YOURSELF

*C*ats play with string. But a Rules cat turns thought-less string-play into works of kinetic art. A Rules cat knows her owner lusts after those moments of Rules cat artistry. The world is your palette. So's the sofa, the chair, the coffee table. Just make sure the yarn is worthy of your talents. Stick to angora, vicuña, and good old cashmere. You're a Rules cat. You have your standards.

Rules, Rules, and More Rules

*W*ith all the hubbub the Rules for Cats has caused—*The Rules* (eww), *The Code* (double eww), even *The Gay* and *Anti Rules* (we'll wait and see), many of our friends and colleagues in the pet kingdom have tried to get in on the act. Here are a few of the books we've been hearing about through the (perfectly pruned) feline grapevine:

The Rules for Snails
Rule 4: Go easy on the salt

The Rules for Vietnamese Potbellied Pigs
Rule 32: Pearls do *not* go before swine

The Rules for Sloths
Rule 11: Be a three-toed creature unlike any other

The Rules for Chia Pets
Rule 7: Don't sprout too fast